WILDLIFE
OF AUSTRALIA

Steve Parish

THE SIGNATURE COLLECTION

Title page: A female Eastern Grey Kangaroo. This kangaroo lives in the woodlands and forests of eastern Australia, in groups called mobs.

Above: The Sugar Glider swoops between trees using the fur-covered membranes that join the fifth finger to the first toe on each side of its body to slow and control its glide.

Two young Eastern Grey Kangaroos play-fighting. This wrestling allows each youngster to establish its rank in the mob. The higher a male's rank, the more females he will mate with.

CONTENTS

INTRODUCTION

In choosing images for this book, I hoped readers would share the wonder I feel when looking at the immense variety and remarkable adaptations of Australia's wildlife. Many of our mammals, birds, reptiles and other creatures exist in habitats that demand forms and lifestyles that have no exact counterparts anywhere else on earth. When someone is faced with a Thorny Devil, a Frilled Lizard, a Platypus, Koala or Short-beaked Echidna for the first time, the thought might spring to mind that this creature could have been invented by a writer of fantasy fiction to inhabit a world in a galaxy far away.

Australia is a vast continent, whose dramatically different habitats provide niches for a great many animals. For millions of years, vast rainforests and inland seas dominated the landmass. Gradually the continent became drier, drought-tolerant plants replaced the rainforests, and then humans arrived, to change whole landscapes by annual burning. The huge animals known as megafauna disappeared. Much later the Dingo made landfall, and when non-indigenous people sailed into Botany Bay in 1788 a new era of land-clearing and importation of animals, including some destructive pests and predators, began.

Today our wildlife is at a turning point. Some species, such as the Common Brushtail Possum and the Red Kangaroo, are doing just fine. Others, such as the Bilby, Numbat and Southern Cassowary, could be headed for extinction if they and their habitats are not protected quickly and absolutely.

Rare or common, often or almost never seen, all of our native animals are precious – and that includes fishes, frogs and insects as well as the more obvious furry, feathery and scaly beasts. Each of them has its own beauty and fascinating habits.

I hope this book will inspire you to go out and look for wild creatures and enjoy them in their natural habitats as well as in nature parks and sanctuaries.

Steve Parish

Opposite: The Red-eyed Tree-frog grows about 6.5 cm long and lives in the forest canopy. It climbs on leaves and branches with the help of adhesive discs on its fingers and toes.

WILDLIFE OF THE BUSHLANDS

INTRODUCTION

"The Bush" is a legendary place in the Australian consciousness – a place of adventure, space, mateship, days spent in hard yakka and nights spent yarning around the campfire. As well as the animals, the distinctive plants of the bush are woven into the legends – gum trees to boil the billy under, mallee roots to negotiate with a stump-jump plough, ti-trees that produce cure-all oil and wattles to be the symbol of our land.

But Australia's bushland animals are legends, each in its own right. There are kangaroos and wombats, Koalas and kookaburras, and a whole swag more. They take their places in a landscape of drought-resistant plants, whose profuse and showy blossoms invite birds, mammals and insects to feed on nectar, thus helping to pollinate the plants. Water may be lacking in the bush but, unlike the deserts hovering on its fringes, there is always a river or a creek or a chain of waterholes somewhere.

When searching for bushland animals, it is helpful to remember that most mammals and frogs are active at night, while birds and reptiles are, on the whole, creatures of the day.

Opposite: A female Eastern Quoll, a cat-sized marsupial predator, with her young ones.

Above: The Shingleback opens its mouth wide to show its blue tongue when it is alarmed.

A sleepy Koala displays the two opposable thumbs that make life in the treetops easier.

Koalas sleep around 20 hours out of each 24, for their diet is a low-energy one.

KOALAS – EUCALYPT CONNOISSEURS

During daylight, a Koala sleeps in the fork of a eucalypt tree, looking from a distance like a large ball of greyish brown fur. If rain falls, it curls up even more tightly and bows its head, letting the downpour simply run off its dense fur. If the sun shines too warmly, the Koala hangs dozing across the branches, limbs asprawl. When the sun sinks, the Koala clambers around its tree, carefully selecting young and tender leaves to eat. Eucalypt leaves are very high in fibre, contain around 50% water, and offer low percentages of starches and protein. They also harbour tannins and other toxic substances. The Koala's 2 m long appendix is home to micro-organisms that help break down leaf fibre. Its liver filters out the poisons. The resulting substances are not very nutritious, but they allow the Koala to have a lifestyle that includes a lot of sleeping and more eating than any other activity.

This Koala is carefully selecting eucalypt leaves to eat. It will choose the choicest and most nutritious growth, avoiding older leaves that are fibrous and difficult to digest.

LOVE AND WAR IN THE TREE TOPS

A male Koala defends his territory from other mature males. He advertises his ownership by bellowing and by rubbing trees with a scented secretion produced on his chest. If another male invades his tree, the resulting battle may be violent. Several females may have their home ranges within reach of a dominant male. When ready to mate, they follow his bellowing. The new-born Koala is bee-sized and must climb to its mother's pouch to survive. It will remain in the pouch for up to seven months, then ride on its mother's back until it becomes independent about one year after birth.

Wedged into a tree fork, this Koala will doze away daylight hours. After nightfall, it will move about the trees in its home range, feeding and sometimes interacting with other Koalas.

Koala fur is composed of densely packed hairs and is water-resistant. A Koala does not make a nest, but relies on its pelt to protect it from sun, wind and rain.

A female Koala will carry her single young one in her pouch for six to seven months, then on her back for a further six months.

SMALL HOPPERS

Kangaroos and their relatives come in a variety of sizes, from huge Red Kangaroos weighing up to 85 kg, down through the wallabies to tiny Musky Rat-kangaroos that weigh a mere 500 g. Second from the bottom in the size ladder are the potoroos and bettongs. Like all of the group, they have powerful hind legs and long feet, with the second and third toes joined together. However, potoroos and bettongs weigh less than 2 kg and eat tubers, fungi and bulbs, which they dig up with their forepaws. They prefer to live in dense undergrowth, emerging at dusk to feed. These tiny marsupials were common when Europeans arrived in Australia. The clearing of their bushy habitat, however, has made them vulnerable to human hunters, foxes, dogs and cats. They have survived only where they are safe from these predators, in sanctuaries such as offshore islands.

This Brush-tailed Bettong is also called by its Aboriginal name of Woylie. It was once very common, but foxes, dogs and clearance of its undergrowth habitat have made it very rare.

The Long-nosed Potoroo plays a useful role in forest growth. Its droppings spread the spores of an underground fungus that helps tree roots get the best food value from poor soil.

A pair of Red-necked Wallabies, one with a joey. Kangaroos and wallabies that live in mobs spend a lot of time in physical interaction, grooming, fighting with or courting each other.

A fast-growing joey makes a burden for this female Eastern Grey Kangaroo. The joey will be carried in the pouch for eleven months, then suckle from outside for another nine months.

GREY KANGAROOS

Grey Kangaroos live where the annual rainfall is more than 250 mm. They prefer to eat grass, and feed from late afternoon to early morning. A big male may measure over 2 m from nose tip to tail tip and weigh up to 66 kg. A female the same age may be only half this weight.

Both start life as a newborn weighing under 1 g. Born after 36 days of gestation, it climbs unaided to the pouch, attaches to a nipple and will not leave the pouch permanently until around 11 months of age. It will then stay with its mother for another six or seven months. By that time, there may be another joey in her pouch, for an embryo held in reserve in her reproductive system will usually have begun to develop as soon as the pouch was vacated.

Young male kangaroos play-fight with their peers, wrestling and kicking to establish their rank in the mob. A dominant male will mate with a large number of females.

Eastern Grey Kangaroos demonstrate one of the advantages of living in a mob – there are plenty of eyes, ears and noses to detect approaching danger. The male is on the right.

BIRDS OF THE BUSHLANDS

Bushland contains many mini-habitats for birds to exploit. Some, such as lorikeets, pardalotes and many honeyeaters, live their lives in the treetops, feasting on nectar and foliage insects. Tree trunks with peeling bark are dining rooms for sittellas, shrike-tits and treecreepers; saplings and bushes provide hunting grounds for robins, fairy-wrens and flycatchers. Where the trees are sparser and there are sufficient patches of grass, parrots waddle seeking seed, Australian Magpies stab and probe for insects, and Laughing Kookaburras snap up unwary reptiles and insects. Waterways and billabongs – especially those bordered with big old trees offering nesting sites – attract cockatoos, magpie-larks, a variety of birds of prey, and hordes of swallows and martins.

A Rainbow Lorikeet drinks nectar from a eucalypt blossom with the aid of its brush-tipped tongue. Native birds help pollinate a large number of Australia's wildflower species.

Cockatoos are large parrots with crests on their heads. This Sulphur-crested Cockatoo has raised and fanned its crest, a sign of excitement, interest or aggression.

IN PARADISE WITH PARROTS

Australia is home to some of the world's most beautiful and unusual parrots. They all have curving bills, the upper mandible attached to the skull by a flexible joint, and they all have two toes directed forwards and two backwards, used like human hands to hold and manipulate objects as well as for climbing.

In size, Australian parrots range from the Palm Cockatoo, huge at around 55 cm, down to the tiny fig-parrots, only about 13 cm. In brilliance of plumage they vary from the sombre black-cockatoos to the gem-like grass-parrots, eye-dazzling female Eclectus and brilliant male Australian King-Parrot. Some, like the Budgerigar, may be seen in thousands in the wild, while the endangered Orange-bellied Parrot may now have a total population of only a few hundred.

Female and immature Australian King-Parrots lack the male's crimson head. They are found in Australia's eastern coastal areas, and feed near forest edges on seed and fruits.

Crimson Rosellas live in forests and woodlands where they eat seed and fruits. A pair mates for life. The female lays up to five white eggs in a tree hollow, then both parents feed the chicks.

TWO DINKUM AUSSIES

The Australian Magpie was named after a British bird, whose name may have come from two words meaning "black and white gossip". "Kookaburra" was an Aboriginal name, recorded by Governor Arthur Phillip in 1789 and used in eastern Australia by indigenous people of many language groups. Both birds eat small creatures, and both have complex family lives. Female magpies live in a group, but take sole responsibility for raising their chicks until the young leave the nest. At this point, other members of the group may assist with feeding them. Male magpies defend territory vigorously. Kookaburras are also territorial; a breeding pair, however, is assisted in bringing up each year's chicks by their family group – unmated young birds from previous breeding seasons.

A group of up to 24 Australian Magpies will defend a territory. At dawn, group members give their carolling call to advertise that they claim a particular area for feeding and nesting.

The Laughing Kookaburra is a large woodland kingfisher that makes a loud, chuckling call at dawn and dusk to claim its territory. The large beak is useful in capturing small creatures, including snakes.

The Common Wombat has a naked nose. It has two rare relatives that have noses ornamented with hair. A large male Common Wombat may weigh up to 39 kg.

A NOT-SO-COMMON WOMBAT

There is nothing common about the large, ground-living Common Wombat. Like other marsupials, the female gives birth to a tiny, naked baby that spends six months in its mother's pouch, then follows her around for nearly another year. The pouch opens to the rear, which is best for baby because a wombat is one of the world's best burrowers. A major burrow may be up to 20 m long, with chambers, side-entrances and even vestibules, where its owner can wait for night to fall before venturing out to find native grasses to eat. Several wombats may share a burrow system.

A young Common Wombat in search of native grasses, shrubs and roots. A wombat may look solid and slow, but, if frightened, can run at up to 40 km/h.

THE PUREBRED DINGO, A VANISHING RACE

The Dingo is a medium-sized wild dog, whose faraway ancestors were probably Indian Wolves. It is a major predator that probably came to northern Australia less than 4000 years ago and rapidly spread throughout the continent. After 1788, human-created sources of water and the population explosion of the rabbit bolstered Dingo numbers, while hunting decimated them. However, the greatest threat to the Dingo's identity is cross-breeding with domestic and feral dogs. In many places in Australia only cross-bred animals exist. The Dingos shown here are certifiably "purebred", for they live on Fraser Island off the coast of Queensland where domestic dogs are not available for interbreeding. Dingos live in packs, which may meet only at intervals. The dominant pair of such a pack breed once a year, while the others help rear the pups.

Opposite and above: These two dingos live on Fraser Island, off the coast of Queensland, one of the few places where dingos have not interbred with domestic or feral dogs.

Sugar Gliders live in groups and identify fellow group members by their scent. They spend the daylight hours in a shared tree hollow, emerging after dark to look for nectar and insects.

POSSUMS AND GLIDERS

Possums, gliders and cuscuses are climbers that feed primarily on tree foliage, fruit flowers and sap. Some groups add a certain amount of insect life to this diet. Gliders, such as the Sugar Glider opposite, have a fur-covered membrane called a patagium stretching between wrists and ankles or wrists and elbows. Once they have gained height, they can leap and use the patagium to glide up to 50 m to another tree. Ringtail possums, such as the one shown below, have two "thumbs" on each hand (like a Koala), grasping hands and feet, and a prehensile tail that acts like a fifth limb. They climb and leap with great agility amongst the tree tops.

The Common Ringtail Possum is found along Australia's eastern coast in forests, woodlands and gardens. It spends the day in a ball-shaped nest, or drey, it has built in dense foliage.

The Short-beaked Echidna is one of only three mammals whose young hatch from eggs laid by the female. This spiky creature eats ants and termites dug from their nests with its claws.

The Diamond Python is harmless to humans but bad news for rats and mice. It tracks prey using its odour-sensitive tongue and the heat-sensitive pits on its lips.

REPTILIAN SUN-WORSHIPPERS

Unlike mammals, which generate their own body heat, reptiles depend on outside factors to provide warmth so their systems can function efficiently. The most popular heat source is the sun, and on sunny mornings scaled creatures from tiny garden lizards to enormous crocodiles may be seen basking to get their muscles and metabolisms ready for action.

Pythons, including the Diamond Python opposite, are a group of non-venomous snakes that kill prey by constriction. When the forked tongue is pulled back, it transfers traces of animals' body heat to an organ in the roof of the snake's mouth. The snake moves towards the fork that retrieved the strongest traces, and so follows the path the prey has taken.

The remarkable skin ruff of the Frilled Lizard serves both to bluff its enemies and as a courtship accessory. It is probably also used to get rid of excessive body heat.

Geckos like the Giant Cave Gecko have soft skins, detachable tails and the hunting instincts of tiny cats. Their eyes look through fixed, transparent lower lids that form "goggles" cleaned by licking.

WILDLIFE OF THE ARIDLANDS

INTRODUCTION

It is a paradox of Australia's aridlands that it is possible to drown in the desert in flash floods that send rain thundering down gorges and rivers. However, it is even more likely that living things will die of heatstroke, dehydration or starvation when drought burns away food plants. Australia has some of the animal kingdom's most drought-combatant creatures, such as frogs that burrow deep when the heat rises, emerging months or even years later when rain returns to the desert. The Thorny Devil below survives on a diet of tiny ants. It need never find open water, for each night its bumpy skin becomes beaded with dew. As mist becomes droplets and droplets become drops, water begins to trickle down channels between the lizard's spikes towards grooves that eventually lead to the corners of its mouth.

The aridlands are full of creatures that exploit the local resources to aid survival and reproduction. The Malleefowl opposite uses the sand's heat to aid its parental duties. The male scratches up a mound of sand and, in it, in a nest chamber lined with vegetation, the female lays egg after egg. Each day the male checks the temperature in the nest until, one by one, the eggs hatch. The chicks fight to the surface, then run away, needing no parental care.

Opposite: The male Malleefowl builds a sand mound then scratches out a nest chamber.

Above: The rubbery spikes on a Thorny Devil's skin help it to obtain drinking water.

A fast-moving male Red Kangaroo. Experiments prove that at speeds above 17 km/h hopping is more efficient in terms of oxygen consumption than running, galloping or bounding.

The Three-lined Knob-tail Gecko hunts insects and reptiles when the sun has set. It remains active when low night temperatures slow down or immobilise other lizards.

BIRDS OF THE ARID INLAND

To survive in the desert, a seed-eating bird must be able to visit a water source at least once each day and preferably more often. Thus cockatoos, pigeons, doves and finches are dependent on waterholes and artesian bores. Birds of prey, such as the majestic Wedge-tailed Eagle, will also be seen near water, for that is where their prey, such as other birds, rabbits or kangaroos, is most easily found.

Major Mitchell's Cockatoo has delicately tinted pink plumage and a scarlet and gold crest. It nests in hollows in large trees and disappears from country where these trees are cut out.

A large female Wedge-tailed Eagle may have a wingspan of 2.3 m. This raptor is often seen soaring, watching the ground below for rabbits or other live prey, or carrion such as roadkill.

Australian Bustards eat grass, seeds and small creatures like mice and grasshoppers. When aware of danger, it freezes, then walks away. The black crown shows that this bird is male.

The Southern Hairy-nosed Wombat lives on the arid Nullarbor Plain. It needs several rainy years, and no competition, to find enough native grasses to wean its young successfully.

THE HABITAT FACTOR

As Australia's climates and landscapes have changed, its native animals have had to develop extremely specialised lifestyles in order to survive. Destroy any element in an environment and some creature will suffer. The two species of hairy-nosed wombats, one of them endangered, cope well with dry conditions so long as there is enough native grass to wean their young. When cattle, sheep or rabbits remove the grass, however, young wombats do not survive to replace their parents.

The Burrowing Bettong has been wiped out in mainland Australia by the clearing of its brushy habitat and the introduction of the fox and feral cat. This small kangaroo-relative now survives only on four tiny islands off north-western Western Australia. The Burrowing Bettong is one of only two kangaroo allies that spends the day in a burrow.

This Burrowing Bettong is an endangered species. It digs burrows as shelters; several burrows may interconnect into a warren inhabited by several animals.

During the day, the Bridled Nailtail Wallaby rests in a hollow it has dug under spinifex. When startled, it hides rather than hops away. It was easy prey for humans and other predators.

The Rufous Hare-wallaby is one of Australia's most endangered mammals. It is now found in the wild only on two small, arid islands in Shark Bay, Western Australia.

CAN THESE ANIMALS BE SAVED?

The Rufous Hare-wallaby (also known as the Mala) and the Bilby are two desert creatures that are on the final few steps of the march to extinction. The Mala was once common in spinifex-covered sand-plains and sand-dune country. Foxes, drought and fire destroyed the final two small mainland groups in the remote Tanami Desert. Now this beautiful wallaby can be seen in the wild only on Bernier and Dorre Islands in Shark Bay, Western Australia. The Lesser Bilby is extinct. The Greater Bilby, a long-eared, soft-furred bandicoot, still exists in tiny colonies in a few isolated desert places. Both wallaby and bilby are being bred in captivity and have been released into their original habitats in controlled and monitored programs. The success of these programs depends on, among other factors, eliminating feral predators and competitors and conserving the vegetation.

The Bilby is a long-eared, soft-furred bandicoot that used to be common in Australia's drier areas and is now very rare. It keeps cool in a burrow during the daytime and feeds at night.

Numbats have high energy requirements and must feed regularly on termites. They are not powerful enough to break into hard termite nests, so they feed from termite runways.

THE ENERGETIC NUMBAT

The termite-eating Numbat is perhaps Australia's most beautiful marsupial. About the size of a small cat, it is bright red-brown, with a darker rump striped white. Its elegant head has a black mask and its long tail fizzes into a quivering bottlebrush when it is moving about. This is Australia's only day-active marsupial, a rare and endangered creature. Living in open woodland, it requires fallen logs in which to shelter, and is vulnerable to fire and predators such as foxes. A Numbat must eat plenty of termites to satisfy the insatiable appetite resulting from its high energy output. Its paws are not powerful enough to break into termite nests, so it must scratch and lick insects from their ground runways and rotting wood. Numbats survive in just a few isolated areas in south-western Australia.

The Numbat takes refuge in a fallen log or hollow stump. It is very wary when emerging to feed, retreating at the least sign of danger.

WILDLIFE OF THE RAINFOREST

INTRODUCTION

Rainforests are plant communities in which the tree crowns almost touch, forming a closed canopy that allows only small amounts of light to filter to the ground. All of these closed forests, whether they grow in tropical or temperate regions, depend upon substantial, regular rainfall. This rainfall encourages the growth of massive trees whose wood is useful to humans. When the forest is logged, its other plants and animals disappear.

Australia's tropical and subtropical rainforest trees are home to mammals such as tree-kangaroos, various possums and cuscuses. Tree trunks and crowns are inhabited by tree-frogs, climbing lizards and snakes; pigeons, parrots and a host of other birds find food and nest sites in the canopy. Fallen logs and leaf-litter form refuges and hunting grounds for other groups of amphibians and reptiles; the giant cassowary, pademelons and wallabies roam the forest floor, picking up fallen fruit and other edibles.

Cool temperate rainforest has its own unique fauna, including the Superb Lyrebird, quolls, gliders and possums, while forest streams harbour the elusive Platypus.

Opposite: The rainforest is home to exquisite creatures such as this Ulysses Butterfly.

Above: A Green Ringtail Possum curls up on the branch of a rainforest tree.

BIRDS OF THE RAINFOREST

The rainforest is home to many birds, but often they are out of sight in the canopy or hidden in the subdued light of the forest floor. The Eclectus and other parrots and pigeons seem strikingly obvious when they perch in the open, but amongst foliage and flowers their brilliant colours blend with their surroundings. The huge, flightless Southern Cassowary can move across the leaf-litter like a shadow. Its presence becomes obvious only when it panics and races off, neck outstretched, its remarkable helmet taking the brunt of encounters with vines and saplings. The male is smaller than the female, and takes responsibility for incubating the eggs and rearing the chicks.

The Southern Cassowary is a large, flightless bird. It exists only in several small, isolated populations in rainforests between Cape York and Townsville, Queensland.

This is a female Eclectus Parrot — her mate has equally brilliant, but green and red, plumage.

These parrots live in the tropical rainforests of far north-eastern Queensland.

The male Regent Bowerbird is resplendent in gold and jet. The female's plumage is less brilliant. He builds a stick avenue, decorates it and sings and dances there to attract her.

THE PLAYBOY AND THE PARTNER

The male Regent Bowerbird maintains the equivalent of a penthouse apartment where macho behaviour and seduction are the order of the day. Once he has had his way with a female attracted both by his bower, with its carefully arranged decorations, and by his singing and posturing, he preens himself while she flies away to build a nest, incubate eggs and bring up the family as conscientiously as any other single mother.

The male Eastern Yellow Robin, on the other hand, sets up housekeeping with his mate in a sedate but tastefully decorated home, then he defends their nest and supports her with carefully selected meals while she sits on their eggs. Once the chicks hatch, he and his mate tend and feed them, often helped by their offspring from previous nestings.

The Eastern Yellow Robin lives on rainforest edges. It is the first bird to call in the morning, well before dawn. A pair claims a territory, where the female builds a bark and cobweb nest.

SEARCH FOR THE REPTILES

Tropical rainforest is an ideal habitat for reptiles because the air is moist and warm all year round; warm temperate rainforest is nearly as hospitable. However, rainforest reptiles are good at concealing themselves and the two shown here are experts in remaining unseen. The Southern Forest Dragon will cling to a tree trunk, its jagged crest and mottled colouring making it appear one with the lichens and mosses around it. The Green Python will coil itself in a tree fork or fern crown and there remain invisible until it chooses to move. It will remain motionless within striking distance of a trail favoured by rainforest mammals until it either secures a victim or decides there is better hunting elsewhere.

The Southern Forest Dragon's rough scales and crest camouflage it amidst the mosses and lichens of the rainforest tree trunks on which it lives.

Until it is 1–3 years old, the Green Python is either yellow or red. Then, quite suddenly, its skin changes colour to a vivid emerald green.

THE TASMANIAN DEVIL

Ever since the last Thylacine died in 1936, the Tasmanian Devil has been Australia's largest marsupial carnivore. It has been confined to Tasmania for the past 400 years, probably eliminated from the mainland by competition from the Dingo. A male Tasmanian Devil weighs around 9–12 kg, a female several kilograms less.

Tasmanian Devils are not sociable animals. Each one will spend the day in its den, under thick bushes, in a hollow log or other sheltered place, then emerge at dusk to hunt insects and other small creatures. Tasmanian Devils eat carrion, and a group will gather around roadkill, squabbling and bickering over the meal. There is much opening of mouths, growling and screeching, but little aggressive contact. In fact, the Devil is usually a timid beast that prefers to trundle away from conflict rather than stand its ground.

Two to four young are born in April. Their mother carries them in her rear-opening pouch for up to 16 weeks, then leaves them in her den. When they are able to, the young follow her while she seeks food, and they are made to fend for themselves by about 40 weeks of age.

Tasmanian Devils are most common in the north-east of the Island State. Since the extinction of the Thylacine, the Devil is the largest marsupial carnivore left in the world.

This gaping display is a Tasmanian Devil's way of telling its fellow Devils that it lays claim to some sort of food — often roadkill. It is not a great killer and prefers to hunt small game.

RAINFOREST FROGS

Although there are plenty of predators eager to catch and consume frogs, the rainforest is a paradise for amphibians. The constant humidity suits their moist, glandular skins and there are plenty of small creatures to eat. Although many species of frog live on the forest floor amongst the leaf-litter, or on the margins of streams, the two shown here are adapted for climbing through the foliage. Their fingers and toes end in discs that adhere to smooth surfaces: some tree-frogs can even climb a pane of glass. Once on a leaf or other flat surface, the frog clings closely so that its underside forms a suction seal with the substrate. It depends on camouflage coloration to hide it from hungry eyes.

When weather conditions are right, male frogs flock to suitable breeding locations and call loudly for mates. This Bleating Tree-frog's vocal sac amplifies his call.

Frogs have delicate, glandular skin that produces antibiotic and antifungal secretions. This is a Red-eyed Tree-frog. The climbing discs on its digits are well displayed in this picture.

On land, a Platypus folds the webbed ends of its digits under, protecting them when it walks or digs its burrow. Eyes and nostrils are on the top of the head and bill.

THE PLATYPUS

When the first Platypus skin to reach England was examined by scientists, they decided such an unlikely creature must be a fake, probably cobbled together from various parts of other creatures. Surely no animal could have a wide, leathery bill, a furry body, a broad tail and webbed feet. It was impossible that a female mammal should lay eggs, or that a male should have venomous spurs on its ankles. When zoologists finally accepted this unlikely creature as real, they called it *Ornithorhynchus anatinus*, which means "duck-like bird-snout".

In more modern times, it has been discovered that the Platypus swims with eyes, ears and nostrils shut, locating the small water creatures on which it feeds by detecting tiny electrical signals from their bodies with special sensors on its bill. It stuffs its cheek pouches with food, then returns to the surface to swallow the prey. The young, having hatched from eggs, suckle milk that oozes onto their mother's abdomen, for she has no nipples.

When a Platypus submerges, the ends of its "fingers" unfold to form webbed paddles. Its body is streamlined and its dense fur is water-resistant, keeping its body dry.

The Platypus can live only in unpolluted fresh water. It cannot dig its burrow where the banks of waterways are trampled and compacted by cattle or other stock.

WILDLIFE OF THE WETLANDS

INTRODUCTION

In Australia, life teems wherever there is plenty of water. In the picture opposite, numerous waterbirds have gathered in one small area of swamp. Obviously there are enough fish, frogs, tadpoles, freshwater crays and aquatic insects to feed the multitude. Wetlands are extremely rich in animal life: in generally arid Australia, rivers, creeks, lakes, swamps, billabongs and estuaries provide habitat for predators and prey alike. In the continent's deserts, few creatures will be visible during times when rain does not fall. However, let storms fill claypans and creek-bed waterholes, and landscapes come to life. Frogs and reptiles emerge from their burrows; birds such as ducks, grebes, stilts, spoonbills and pelicans fly in to plunder the water plants, fishes and shrimps that appear in the water as if by magic. Frogs, turtles, snakes and lizards, birds and desert mammals breed while water and abundant food are available. Nowhere is this transformation more marked than on the wetlands of the far north of the continent, where seasonal monsoon rains flood rivers and plains and the landscape comes alive with phenomenal numbers of birds, fishes, aquatic snakes, turtles – and crocodiles.

Opposite: Egrets wade through the shallows, seeking fish, frogs and crustaceans.

Above: The Northern Dwarf Tree-frog breeds in wetlands vegetation in northern Australia.

The Saltwater Crocodile lives in coastal waterways and wetlands in northern Australia. This one is basking beside a tropical lagoon, digesting its latest meal.

BIRDS BATHING

Meticulous care of the plumage is essential for all birds, and waterbirds are particularly careful of their feathers. The stiffest outer feathers that protect the body and form the flying feathers of the wings and tail have a unique structure. Each filament, or barb, on either side of the central vane is linked to the next by rows of tiny hooks that hold together like the teeth on a zipper. At intervals during the day, a bird turns its head about on its flexible neck and preens its plumage, running the bill down the feathers and locking disarranged barbs back together again. Every few strokes, the bird, especially if it is a waterbird, will take oil from a preen gland on its rump (a chicken's "parson's" or "pope's nose") and spread the waterproofing oil through its plumage. Some birds, such as egrets and herons, have special feathers that fray into a powder that they spread through the plumage.

Waterfowl such as Burdekin Shelducks spend much of their time bathing and preening their plumage. They waterproof their feathers with oil from a gland above the tail.

The Yellow-billed Spoonbill preens its back feathers with its spatulate bill. When a spoonbill is swishing its bill from side to side in water, the tip snaps up prey in a fraction of a second.

The Darter has a trigger mechanism in the kink of its long, sinuous neck that flicks the head forward explosively to spear fish on its sharp bill.

HUNTERS AND GATHERERS

Waterbirds come in a variety of shapes.

Long-necked, long-legged, long-billed stalkers, such as herons, egrets, storks, stilts, avocets, ibis and spoonbills, snap up their prey from shallow water or swampy grassland. Some egrets and herons may grab victims from a hunting perch just above water level.

Short-legged, rubbery-billed paddlers such as ducks and swans dive or suzzle for waterweed around the water's margins. Geese, with their longer legs and harder, edged beaks, crop and graze their way across waterside pasture.

Underwater hunters such as cormorants, the Darter and grebes have legs set far back on their bodies and webbed or lobed toes. These act as propellers in the water.

A Black-necked Stork, or Jabiru, is oblivious to the ghostly trail of its mate's flight captured by the camera. It is the only stork found in Australia.

Australian Pelicans may appear on fresh or salt water anywhere in inland Australia, or along its coasts, where there are fish to catch in their massive bills.

WILDLIFE OF THE COASTS

INTRODUCTION

Australia is supremely lucky in having a wonderfully lengthy and varied coastline. Circling the continent, one can travel past sandy or pebbly beaches, rocky headlands, mangrove mudflats, sheer limestone cliffs and, amongst other spectacular features, some of the world's most magnificent coral reefs.

Coastal habitats consist of three distinct zones. There is the region below the low tideline, the realm of fishes and countless numbers of other lifeforms, a watery world that air-breathing creatures visit only if they are well-adapted to make a living there. There is the intertidal zone, where animal life has to contend with twice-daily submersion alternating with exposure to the atmosphere. And there is the area above normal high tide, submerged only in exceptional circumstances, usually covered in sand or sea-shaped rock, a region influenced by both ocean and land.

Each environment has its own creatures, and a wondrous lot they are. The sea was the cradle of life on earth, and contains representatives of nearly every major form of animal life. Amphibians, with their water-absorbing skins, are absent, but air-breathing mammals, reptiles and birds all live in, or find their food in, the ocean.

Opposite: Schooling fish find safety in numbers.

Above: The Lionfish defends itself with venomous spines that cause great pain.

The muscular power of a Bottlenose Dolphin's tail allows it to hold its head out of the water in an action called "spy-hopping" that allows it a view of its above-water surroundings.

DOLPHINS – FRIENDLY SEA-DWELLERS

It is believed that dolphins were once land mammals. Over a long period they returned to the ocean, their limbs became adapted for swimming and their bodies for survival in the sea. Eventually they could no longer live on land. They lost much, but amongst the gains were the ability to send out sound and to learn from the returning echoes the composition and identity of any object in the path of the noise.

On many places around Australia's coasts, pods of Bottlenose Dolphins regularly patrol beaches and bays, hunting for fish and other marine creatures. Sometimes a group of these streamlined mammals will visit a beach and allow people to approach them closely. The dolphins form a marked contrast with their human fellow-mammals. Their breathing passages open through a blowhole on the top of the head, their hind limbs are not visible, their fore limbs are flippers and their tails end in powerful swimming flukes. However, their bodies function in the same way as human bodies, they feed their young on milk and their survival, like that of humans, depends on regular deep breaths of air.

Bottlenose Dolphins learn about things in the water around them by echolocation. A dolphin emits high-pitched sounds that bounce back from an object and give information about it.

Under water, an Australian Fur-seal swims with effortless grace amongst the Giant Kelp of Bass Strait. This mammal's fur coat is dense and water-repellent.

SEALS AND SEA-LIONS

The smooth outline of a seal's body comes from a layer of fat called blubber that overlies the muscle. Besides keeping the seal warm in the cold seas, the blubber streamlines the body, helping it move through water. Both fur-seals and sea-lions belong to a group called "eared seals": on land, they prop themselves up on their fore flippers and can also use their hind flippers to lever themselves along. However, in the sea they are transformed into speedy aquabats, moving through the ocean with the grace and agility of fishes.

A female Australian Sea-lion basks in the sun on a southern Australian beach. Sea-lions were hunted nearly to extinction by humans; their numbers are slowly rebuilding.

A school of Moses Perch shelters under a coral overhang on Queensland's Great Barrier Reef. Some fishes are active by day, while others come out to feed at night.

FISHES IN ALL THEIR VARIETY

All fishes breathe by gulping in water then passing it out again over gills that extract oxygen and pass waste gases into the water. The earliest fishes, which roamed the world's oceans 500 million years ago, had neither jaws nor teeth. By 400 million years ago, there were fishes with jaws and armoured scales. In the time since, their various tribes have increased and diversified to inhabit every saltwater and freshwater niche possible.

The Great Barrier Reef and the waters of north-west Western Australia are home to large numbers of fascinating fishes. More temperate seas around Australia's coasts may not contain so many species, but are even richer in individual fish numbers.

The Pink Anemonefish shelters in the stinging tentacles of a sea anemone. It is covered with a special mucus that allows it to become desensitised to the tentacles' stings.

FEATHERED SEAFARERS

For a feathered flier to catch its food underwater requires skill and sometimes physical modifications. Penguins have given up flight in air altogether, and fly through the water using their flippers as wings. Cormorants swim well, but need to spend long periods perched, wings open, drying their feathers and warming up the chilly fish they have swallowed. Terns, noddies, boobies and gannets plunge-dive to catch fish under water, but seldom alight on the water. The Australian Pelican does not plunge but swims on the surface, scooping up scaly prey with the aid of its long neck and huge, pouch-bottomed bill.

The Little Penguin is the smallest of a group of flippered, web-footed seabirds. It nests on Australia's southern shore, going to sea at dawn to catch fish and squid for its two chicks.

Roseate Terns are seabirds that catch surface fish by hovering on their long, slender wings above the water, then plunge-diving to seize a victim. They nest on coral cays and islands.

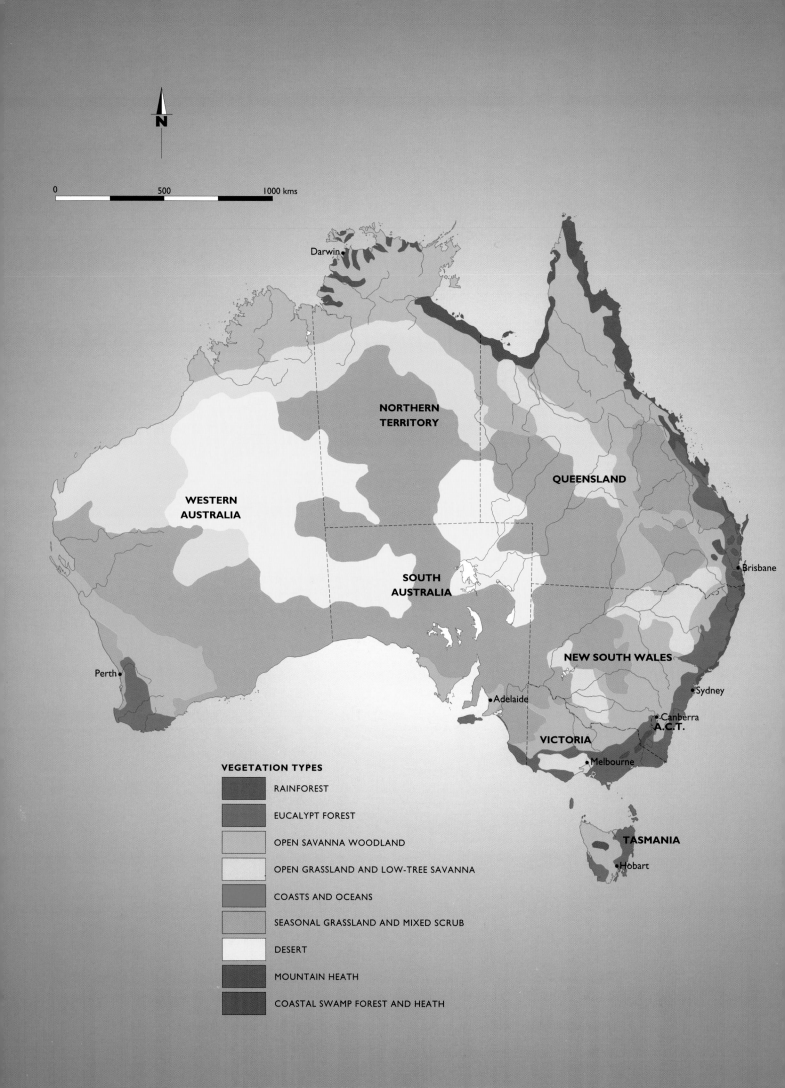

N

0   500   1000 kms

Darwin •

**NORTHERN
TERRITORY**

**WESTERN
AUSTRALIA**

QUEENSLAND

• Brisbane

**SOUTH
AUSTRALIA**

NEW SOUTH WALES

• Sydney

• Adelaide

• Canberra
A.C.T.

VICTORIA

• Melbourne

TASMANIA

• Hobart

Perth •

VEGETATION TYPES

RAINFOREST

EUCALYPT FOREST

OPEN SAVANNA WOODLAND

OPEN GRASSLAND AND LOW-TREE SAVANNA

COASTS AND OCEANS

SEASONAL GRASSLAND AND MIXED SCRUB

DESERT

MOUNTAIN HEATH

COASTAL SWAMP FOREST AND HEATH

DISCOVERING WILDLIFE

The discovery of wild creatures is one of the greatest adventures that Australia can offer. Many of the continent's animals, especially its mammals, are quite different from creatures seen anywhere else in the world, and the ways in which they interact with each other and their habitats are truly amazing.

To appreciate how remarkable Australia's animals are, it helps to travel about looking at the environments they live in, from rainforest to reef, and from snow-covered alpine peaks to red deserts. Best of all is discovering the harmony between an animal and its environment. A Rainbow Lorikeet visiting brilliant blossom in a eucalypt or grevillea, a Green Python coiled in an equally green rainforest fern, a Marbled Velvet Gecko on a bar of striped jasper, a muscular Red Kangaroo hopping across red earth, a Numbat peering from a hollow Wandoo log – each is a rare gem in an equally precious setting.

The Marbled Velvet Gecko lives in drier parts of Australia. It spends daylight hours under bark, or in a crevice in rock or tree, and emerges to hunt insects and spiders at night.

INDEX